ECOLOGY WATCH

GRASSLANDS

Alan Collinson

Cloverleaf
An imprint of Evans Brothers Limited

Cloverleaf is an imprint of Evans Brothers Limited

Evans Brothers Limited
2A Portman Mansions
Chiltern Street
London W1M 1LE

First published 1992

Typeset by Fleetlines Typesetters, Southend-on-Sea
Printed in Spain by GRAFO, S.A. – Bilbao

ISBN 0 237 51206 8

Acknowledgements

Editor: Su Swallow
Design: Neil Sayer
Production: Jenny Mulvanny

Illustrations: David Gardner, Graeme Chambers
Maps: Hardlines, Charlbury

For permission to reproduce copyright material the author
and publishers gratefully acknowledge the following:

Cover (Wildebeest under rainy season sky, Kenya) Richard
Packwood, Oxford Scientific Films
Title page (Tourists viewing zebra, Kenya) Anthony
Bannister/NHPA

p4 Leonard Lee Rue, Bruce Coleman Limited **p5** Dr Morley
Read, Science Photo Library, (inset) Fredy Mercay, Bruce
Coleman Limited **p6** N. Callow/NHPA, (inset) G.I. Bernard,
Oxford Scientific Films **p7** Stan Osolinski, Oxford
Scientific Films **p8** Kathie Atkinson, Oxford Scientific
Films **p9** Carol Hughes, Bruce Coleman Limited **p10**
Richard Packwood, Oxford Scientific Films **p11** David C.
Fritts, Oxford Scientific Films **p12** David Tomlinson/NHPA
p13 Mark Boulton, Bruce Coleman Limited **p14** (top &
bottom) Martin Wendler/NHPA **p15** (left) Keith Gunnar,
Bruce Coleman Limited, (right) Gerald Cubitt, Bruce
Coleman Limited **p16** (top) Kathie Atkinson, Oxford
Scientific Films, (bottom) Jane Burton, Bruce Coleman
Limited **p17** (from top) (1) Ralph & Daphne Keller/NHPA,
(2) Anthony Bannister/NHPA, (3) Sinclair Stammers,
Science Photo Library, (4) Mark Boulton, Bruce Coleman
Limited **p18** (top) Dr Norman Myers, Bruce Coleman
Limited, (bottom) Gunter Ziesler, Bruce Coleman Limited
p19 L.C. Marigo, Bruce Coleman Limited **p20** Okapia,
Oxford Scientific Films **p21** Mark Edwards/Still Pictures
p22 John Cooke, Oxford Scientific Films **p23** John
Markham, Bruce Coleman Limited, (inset) Richard
Anthony, Holt Studios Photograph Library **p24** (top &
bottom) Gunter Ziesler, Bruce Coleman Limited **p25**
Stephen Krasemann/NHPA **p26** Jeff Foott, Bruce Coleman
Limited **p27** Sarah Errington, Hutchison Library **p28** (top
& bottom) L.C. Marigo, Bruce Coleman Limited, (middle)
Dr Morley Read, Science Photo Library **p29** John Shaw/
NHPA **p30** Mary Evans Picture Library **p31** The Vintage
Magazine Company **p33** Jeff Foott, Bruce Coleman
Limited **p34** John Shaw/NHPA **p35** Hutchison Library
p36 ECOSCENE/Sally Morgan **p37** Leonard Lee Rue, Bruce
Coleman Limited **p38** (top) Anthony Bannister, Oxford
Scientific Films, (bottom) John Shaw/NHPA **p39**
ECOSCENE/Sally Morgan **p40** Erwin & Peggy Bauer, Bruce
Coleman Limited **p41** Hutchison Library, (inset) Leonard
Lee Rue, Bruce Coleman Limited **p42** (top) Peter Jackson,
Bruce Coleman Limited, (bottom) Jen & Des Bartlett, Bruce
Coleman Limited **p43** Peter Jackson, Bruce Coleman
Limited **p44** Roger Tidman/NHPA

Contents

Introduction

△ Grasses such as oats are cultivated for food.

About five million years ago on the grassy plains of Africa an animal evolved that was destined to become the world's most important animal. The animal was the first ancestor of ourselves. Our ancestors soon spread to other kinds of environment, such as forests, mountains and deserts. For nearly all the time humans have lived on the Earth, they have had to depend for all their needs on what the environment provided. They gathered the edible plant material and hunted the animals. Because the number of people could not increase beyond what the Earth provided naturally, people and the Earth's resources were in balance. About 10,000 years ago this balance changed dramatically. People learned how to breed and cultivate crops and how to domesticate animals. Many of the most important crops

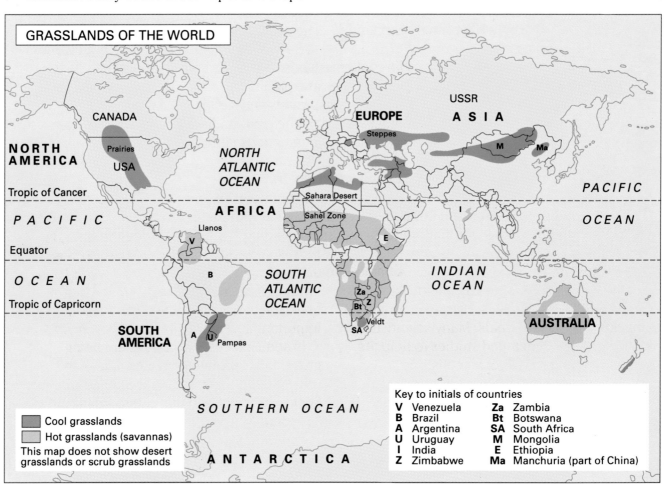

GRASSLANDS OF THE WORLD

NORTH AMERICA
CANADA
Prairies
USA
Tropic of Cancer

NORTH ATLANTIC OCEAN

PACIFIC

EUROPE
Steppes

USSR
ASIA
M   Ma

PACIFIC

Sahara Desert
AFRICA
Sahel Zone

OCEAN

Llanos
V

Equator

B

E

I

INDIAN OCEAN

OCEAN
Tropic of Capricorn

SOUTH ATLANTIC OCEAN

Za
Bt Z
Veldt
SA

AUSTRALIA

SOUTH AMERICA
A U Pampas

SOUTHERN OCEAN

Cool grasslands
Hot grasslands (savannas)
This map does not show desert grasslands or scrub grasslands

Key to initials of countries

V	Venezuela	Za	Zambia
B	Brazil	Bt	Botswana
A	Argentina	SA	South Africa
U	Uruguay	M	Mongolia
I	India	E	Ethiopia
Z	Zimbabwe	Ma	Manchuria (part of China)

ANTARCTICA

△ Grasslands are found in every continent of the world, from Australia (inset) to South America (main picture).

were the grasses, such as wheat, rice, maize, barley and oats. Most of the farm animals were also dependent on the grasses for their food. Since then more and more grassland has been converted to farmland, largely because of the rich soils produced in grassland areas.

Ecology, the study of plants and animals in relation to their surroundings, can tell us not only of the damage we are causing to different environments, but also how we can avoid such damage and how we can restore the land to good heart again. Nowhere is this ecological knowledge more important than in the world's grasslands. Here, in Africa especially, is the greatest reserve of large backboned land animals. Many scientists are carrying out detailed studies to help the animals' survival. Other scientists are studying the plants themselves and how to preserve their variety into the future. This variety can be very important in helping us directly as well as helping the animals.

Many of our food crops have been bred to produce varieties that give big yields. But these varieties have lost many of the characteristics of the wild plants from which they come. As grasslands disappear, so the wild plants are disappearing. This means that the plant genes (which determine characteristics that can be inherited) are being lost. Among these genes there may be ones that can provide disease resistance, or resistance to drought or to poor soil or other natural hazards to growth. These genes could be bred into our crop plants – genetic engineering has already produced stronger varieties of wheat, maize and rice. To keep such characteristics, seeds from wild plants are gathered and preserved in 'gene banks'. The gene banks are some of the most important developments of modern science.

In some places, the grasses are being grown in an effort to recreate some of the original types of grassland (see page 32). Such schemes mean that grasslands – and the animals that live there – will have an increasing chance of survival in the future.

Words printed in **bold** are explained at the end of each section.

Grasses – a success story

Simple means strong

It is not always easy to see the differences between grasses of different species. They do not have bright flowers, they are not woody, they do not grow very big, they all have similar leaves, and when they are crowded together it is even difficult to tell one individual plant from another. Yet these fairly simple plants are found growing abundantly in all sorts of climates and conditions. They cover large areas of the Arctic as well as the hot tropical lands. They are found from the sea edge to the highest mountain tops. One type even grows on sandy sea beds where seaweed cannot hold on. In fact, before people changed the world's landscapes by farming, grasses covered about one quarter of all the Earth's land. How is it that grasses can grow so well in so many different places? The reasons are found in the way they are linked with their surroundings, that is, their ecology.

Blown on the wind

The first reason for the success of grasses lies in how they reproduce themselves. Grasses are flowering plants but unlike most flowering plants, they do not have brightly coloured petals or complicated flower shapes to attract insects to **pollinate** them. The grasses are pollinated by the wind. Because grasses are not dependent on local populations of suitable insects for their reproduction, they can colonise new lands more easily. Also, the pollen can be blown to plants nearby or plants quite a long way away.

These are not the only advantages of wind pollination. Grasses do not have to use their food resources to make complex flowers to attract insects, so they have more food to

▷ Grasses have spikes of small flowers (far right), with no petals. The stamens, which hang from the flower, produce the pollen, which is easily shaken out by the wind (inset).

produce other kinds of growth such as denser roots and more shoots. This means that they can grow quite fast.

Many grasses can also reproduce rapidly by producing new plants from old ones. This is called vegetative reproduction. Some do this by means of underground stems (rhizomes), some by producing new plants at the end of long shoots. Many kinds of grass can go on reproducing like this for years without producing any flowers or seeds at all.

Surviving drought

Wind pollination and vegetative reproduction alone are not sufficient to explain the success of the grasses. Many other plants are wind-pollinated, including many trees, and many plants use vegetative reproduction. To explain why grasses have

covered so much land we have to look for other reasons. Climate is the most important reason why different parts of the world have different kinds of vegetation (plant cover).

The Earth's land vegetation in middle and low **latitudes** is divided into three main types: forest, grassland and **scrubland**. Where land is well-watered forests grow. Where there is a long dry season many grasslands are found. And where the rainfall is low or very unreliable there is scrubland. (Scrubland may also have very large amounts of grass.)

The relationship between plant cover and water supply seems quite simple at first. The grasses are well fitted to resist drought. Their leaves are packed close together so water

▽ Hot grassland with trees in Tanzania in East Africa

loss is cut down, they have dense roots which may form turf and hold water, and many of their stems are underground. Grasses are therefore well adapted to trapping rainwater before it has time to penetrate underground. The turf cover and close-packed leaves hold the water near the surface well. This means that deeper-rooted plants, such as trees and bushes, cannot get enough water to grow as rapidly as the grasses. However, many of these deeper-rooted plants can tap water lower down in the ground, which the grass roots cannot reach. Many of them are also as well adapted to drought as the grasses are. Even though trees grow slowly, they could eventually rise above the grasses and shade them out or reduce their growth. So climate alone cannot explain why grasses are so successful. The factor that gives grasses an extra advantage is that, unlike many other plants, being eaten by animals can make them grow faster.

The first grazers

Widespread grasslands did not exist on the Earth until about 20 million years ago – there were none at the time of the dinosaurs, for instance. Before that time the Earth was very warm and damp and animals fed mainly on the softer leaves of bushes, trees and flowers. Many of these early animals became extinct when the climate became cooler and the interior of the continents became drier. This gave the grasses a chance to spread. They were helped by animals that began to depend on them for food. These first grazers were various kinds of ungulates (hoofed mammals). Twenty million years ago in Asia, for example, great herds of the three-toed horse *Hipparion* roamed the extensive grasslands. These animals were descended from horses that lived in the forests rather than on open grasslands.

As the landscapes became more grassy and open, the need for swiftness to escape predators became important. In Africa, Asia and North America, the larger heavier grazing animals were hunted by predators such as a huge sabre-toothed cat. Smaller cats as well as dogs hunted the smaller grazers. In **Eurasia** hyenas, some as big as

△ Kangaroos can move swiftly on the grasslands in Australia.

the modern lion, hunted down their prey in large packs. To escape these hungry carnivores, the grazers became lighter and swifter.

The modern grazers

Within the group of hoofed animals which became adapted to grassland life are two main branches: the artiodactyls – ungulates with hooves with an even number of toes, and the perissodactyls – ungulates with an odd number of toes on their hooves. The artiodactyls include hippopotamuses, pigs, camels, deer, antelopes, cattle, goats and sheep. The perissodactyls include horses, zebras, rhinoceroses, giraffes and tapirs. All these animals evolved teeth which were suited to grinding up the tough leaves of the grasses and not the softer leaves of forest trees, flowers or marshy plants. In times of drought, however, they not only ate the drought-resistant grasses but also any woody plants that appeared. Their feeding destroyed the woody plants but not the grasses, which are little damaged by grazing. Cutting off the tops of the grass leaves allows the sun in to the lower parts of the plant, which can then grow from shoots near the ground even more strongly. Thus the herds of grazing animals and the grasses evolved together towards our present kinds of grasslands. In some parts of the world such as Africa the relationship between grasses and animals has become very close. Experiments have shown that, for example, the saliva of certain animals actually stimulates the grass to grow faster.

The reasons for the success of the grasslands that we have looked at so far go a long way to explaining their land cover on the map. However, there are many areas of these lands which trees could occupy if it were not for three 'dangerous allies' of the grasses. These are fire, ice and humans. In the next chapter we will see how two of these allies have given the grasses even greater advantages.

pollinate – transfer pollen from the male anthers to the female stigma of a flower so that seeds can form.
latitudes – (here) regions at a certain distance from the equator.
scrubland – land covered in bushes and stunted trees.
Eurasia – the continents of Europe and Asia.

▽ Zebras at a waterhole in southwest Africa. In the dry season, zebras and other animals that live in the hot grasslands of Africa often have to migrate to find water.

Fire and ice

Fire for life

We tend to think of forest fires as dangerous accidents, always to be avoided. But fire is one of the most important natural events in the life of plants. Without it many kinds of vegetation would not easily renew their growth. Fire clears away dead material on trees and bushes and plant **litter** on the ground. The burning of old leaves, stems and other matter releases plant foods which are washed into the soil. These plant foods are then taken up by roots and new growth is produced.

Fire can occur in almost any kind of vegetation if the plants are close enough together for the fire to travel easily. Even the wet tropical jungles can have forest fires. A fire may be started by lightning, volcanic eruption, or even by grains of sand acting as tiny lenses concentrating the Sun's rays. Fire is so naturally a part of the ecology of many plants that they have developed fire resistance to survive it. The eucalyptus trees of Australia, for example, produce buds that are protected against fire. Some plants actually need fire to encourage their growth. The black spruce in the United States, for example, has cones which have to be scorched by fire before they will open to release their seeds.

Most plants are not so reliant upon fire for their success as the black spruce is.

△ An African grass that flourishes after fire

▽ Fire helps to keep out woody plants that would compete with the grasses.

△ Arctic tundra in Alaska, a treeless landscape which contains grassland

Nevertheless, in regions where a dry season allows fires to occur frequently, most plants need to be fire resistant in order to survive. The grasses are well suited to life in these regions. They have underground stems, tightly protected buds and they produce much less standing dry vegetation than trees. This means that the fires tend to be less hot, and less damaging to the grass buds. When the rains come, the grasses are soon putting out new, healthy, green shoots. At the same time tree seeds that have survived the fire are germinating as well. The new plant growth is soon gobbled up by the grazers, but while the tree seedlings are killed off, the grasses flourish from the grazing. So once again, the grasses triumph over their rivals for territory!

The ice ages

About two million years ago, the climate of the world became very much colder. The ice sheets of the Arctic advanced southwards, covering large areas of North America, Europe and northern Asia. The period of ice ages had begun. Geologists name this time (two million to 10,000 years ago) the Pleistocene epoch. During the Pleistocene epoch the ice sheets advanced at least six times, with milder periods called interglacials in between. Sometimes the climate of the interglacials was much milder than the climate we have now. Such drastic changes of climate had many effects on the world's vegetation and animals.

New land for the grasses

Before the ice ages began forest covered large areas of the northern hemisphere. In North America and eastern Asia the forest trees were able to migrate southwards to escape the colder climate. But in Europe the way to safety was blocked by the Mediterranean Sea. Here, most of the forest was gradually destroyed as one glacial period followed another.

△ A steppe landscape in Kazakhstan. These are dry grasslands with unreliable rainfall.

The destruction of the forests and a drier climate allowed the hardy grasses to occupy much larger territories. Two kinds of grassland developed. The first type grew near the edge of the ice. This cold land was colonised by a mixture of plants which had already become hardy in high mountains. This type of vegetation is called **tundra** and the plants are known as arctic-alpine plants. The other type of grassland was what is now called **steppe**, or prairie.

In the low latitudes, the climate during the ice ages remained warm but rainfall patterns altered. Many areas which had been desert became grassland, and former grasslands were covered by trees.

New challenges for the animals

The shifting of the vegetation zones that occurred during the ice ages altered the living conditions for many animals. Those animals that lived in the northern hemisphere, near the ice sheets, had to adapt in order to survive or else perish and become extinct. For example, until the ice ages the giraffe-camels were a common group in North America. But after the destruction of the forests their food supply disappeared and they became extinct. Other animals adapted to the colder conditions and the different vegetation. Many evolved thicker fur, new kinds of blood circulation, and a larger bulk in order to retain more body heat. Many of the animals migrated long distances to avoid the cold winters.

The megafauna

Large size was such an advantage in the cold climate of the ice ages that many groups of animals grew bulkier. In the Americas, the giant sloth *Megatherium* was as large as a modern elephant. In Eurasia a gigantic rhinoceros called *Elasmotherium* evolved. Its horn was up to two metres long. In Australia the giant kangaroo named *Procoptodon* stood up to three metres high. Some animals from before the ice ages were already large enough to survive the change in climate. The woolly elephant-like mastodons, or mammoths, lived throughout the Pleistocene epoch. Feeding on these animals were huge carnivores such as the sabre-toothed cats, such as *Smilodon*. Geologists have named this collection of large animals a 'megafauna' ('large animals').

The beginning of the modern world

The end of the megafauna came when the glaciers began to retreat once more, between 12,000 and 10,000 years ago. However, the change of climate may not have been the only reason for their extinction. There is plenty of evidence that a far worse predator than the sabre-toothed tiger helped to speed them on their way. By this time people were hunting them down. Human beings were beginning to change the face of the Earth almost as much as the forces of nature had in the past. The grasses had found a new and even more dangerous ally than fire and ice.

▷ Not all savanna animals eat grass. The giraffe feeds mainly on tree leaves.

litter – (here) layer of rotting plant material.

tundra – a vast treeless area of land in the Arctic.

steppe – a vast grassy plain with no or few trees.

The tropical grasslands

The savannas

When the Spanish first came to the Americas in the 1500s, they found large areas of grassland in the interior of South America. They also found that the Indians of the region had a name for them. The word was adopted by the Spanish and is now a general term used around the world to describe hot grasslands, the savannas. They are found in Africa, South America, Australia, the Indian sub-continent and southeast Asia. In the last two areas, centuries of farming have changed the nature of the vegetation so much that only a few areas can be considered to be 'natural'. Many of the 'savannas' of these regions are the result of clearing the land for agriculture, which has destroyed the original forests. Natural

Savanna in Brazil, South America, in the dry season (above, a lake shrinking) and flooded in the rainy season (below)

savanna lands cover about one fifth of the world's land surface. They are where some of the most rapid growth of human population is taking place. They also contain some of the last true wildernesses in nature, with some of the largest wild animal herds.

What is savanna?

To define exactly what makes a savanna landscape is not easy. It may be covered by trees and bushes, or be completely open. It may be natural, or manmade by burning. It can have high rainfall, or only very little rain. It can be found on all sorts of different soils. However, its one dominant character, whatever it is like in detail, is that a large part of its surface will be covered by grass plants.

In the savannas, the grasses growing at any particular place are usually dominated by only one or two species. The range of different heights of these tropical grasses is usually much greater than would be found in cool grasslands or cultivated grasses. At one extreme, in the wetter regions where there is a short dry season, the plants may be several metres high. In Africa the elephant grass can grow up to three or four metres high, tall enough to hide an elephant, hence its name. On lands with a long dry season and unreliable rainfall, the grass may be sparse and short. In most of the savannas, which are neither very wet nor very dry, the grass is about one metre high. However, in places where animals graze the grass can be reduced to quite short grazing lawns. All the grasses are adapted to drought (see page 7) and most have underground stems.

Trees in the savannas

In most savannas many kinds of trees and shrubs grow above the grass layer. Many of these trees and shrubs have evolved similar adaptations to the grasses in order to survive a dry season. They have long roots to tap underground water. Their tops are often flattened so as to present as little resistance as possible to the wind, which could dry them out. Most have small, hard leaves which they shed during the dry season. Some, like the baobab tree, are bottle-shaped to store water. Most have thick, protective bud scales and bark. These not only help to keep water inside but also resist that dangerous ally of the grass, fire.

△ Elephant grass needs plenty of water, so it is found in areas with high rainfall.

▷ The Acacia Karoo, from South Africa, produces more than 20,000 seeds each year.

All the savanna plants produce large numbers of seeds. One African acacia tree makes over 20,000 seeds a year, nearly all of them fertile. The savanna plants need to produce so many seeds because very few of them ever get the chance to grow into new plants. Most are eaten by termites, birds or grazing animals, or are destroyed by fire.

Savanna formations

Different kinds of vegetation are divided by ecologists into 'formations'. These are grouped together as formation-types. The savanna is a formation-type which contains four main different savanna formations. These are all found in the three southern continents where natural savannas are most widespread: South America, Africa and Australia. They are:

1) grassland savanna where trees cover less than one per cent of the surface.

2) savanna parkland where trees cover up to 10 per cent of the surface.

3) dense savanna with trees covering between 10 and 50 per cent of the surface.

4) savanna woodland with trees covering between 50 and 90 per cent of the surface, and shrubs and grass as the ground layer.

△ A termite savanna in Australia

▽ Each termite species builds its own nest type.

Termite nests

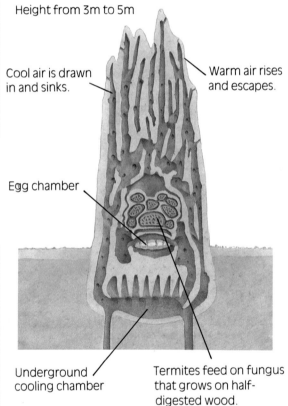

The nest is built of fine soil particles, glued with saliva and faeces.

Height from 3m to 5m

Cool air is drawn in and sinks.

Warm air rises and escapes.

Egg chamber

Underground cooling chamber

Termites feed on fungus that grows on half-digested wood.

△ A termite mound is air-conditioned. Warm air escapes through small pores in the walls, while other pores allow cool air to enter.

When a mound is abandoned, the rich fine soil is spread by the rain and encourages plant growth.

△ Savanna formations: (from top) grassland with almost no trees in Australia, parkland savanna in Namibia, dense savanna with trees covering up to 50 per cent of the surface in Swaziland, Africa, and savanna woodland in Zambia.

What grows where

The kind of formation that develops at any one place is the result of at least five deciding factors: climate, soil, grazing, fire, and ground water. All these factors act together to create the ecological conditions. If there is high rainfall then trees are likely to flourish. But if there is a good growth of trees then fires will be hotter which, in turn, will do more damage to the trees. The climate may also influence when the fires are likely to occur, and, as a result, how devastating they will be. Cool season fires are less damaging than hot season fires, but the hot season is usually the rainy season too, so fires may be less likely then anyway. After a fire the type of soil will affect the regrowth of the plants. In a region where the soil allows water through easily, plant food released from the ash left after the fires may be washed down into the soil. Tree roots can then reach it more easily than the grass roots. If the soil is denser and does not allow water to sink through it the plant food may be blown away, or it may stay near the surface where the grass can feed off it.

In Zambia in 1933, near a town named Ndola, the British forest service chose three large areas of savanna woodlands for an experiment. They set fire to these areas every year at different times. One area was burned at the end of the dry season to give a hot fire. A second area was fired at the start of the dry season to give a cool fire, and a third was protected from fire altogether. By 1944 all the

Leopards (above) and lions (left) find shade and shelter in the trees and grass of the savanna.

trees had gone from the first area, but the second had retained all its plant species. The third area had become a closed evergreen forest. There was virtually no grass layer left. Another experiment in the Olokenji Forest Reserve in Nigeria produced similar results.

Experiments like these are very important because they help ecologists to understand how to conserve the vegetation, and the animals which depend on it. In the Zambian experiment, almost all the grassland animals had disappeared from the area of woodland which was completely protected from fire, and there were fewer animals in the savanna that had lost all its trees. The trees are important because they provide shade and shelter for animals. It is also essential that an area of savanna should have a variety of grasses, because the different animal species usually prefer different kinds of grass. This is not only for food. Many African animals use long grass to hide their young when they are born.

Farming on savanna soils

In hot climates the insects, earthworms, fungi and bacteria are all active in releasing plant food from dead material. If there is sufficient water, the plants take up this food very quickly. If they did not do this the food would soon be washed out of the soil by the torrential rains which occur frequently in tropical lands. As a result there is not a large reserve of food retained in the soil itself.

When people clear the land for their crops, and then harvest the plants they have grown, they are removing the plant food with the crops. This means that the soil must either have heavy dressings of fertiliser, or be abandoned to natural vegetation. The natural plants can then build up the plant food again, a process that may take many years. In Africa and parts of South America

▽ Gauchos (cowboys) herd sheep and cattle on the pampas grasslands of South America.

this natural plant food is used by the farmers who practise subsistence farming. They grow food for themselves and for their families to eat with little or no surplus left over. Crops cannot usually be grown on the same soil for more than three years. It may then take between 10 and 25 years to build up the plant food again. So the fields are constantly moved around. This sort of farming is called bush fallowing, shifting agriculture, or sometimes slash and burn farming. Successful crop farming of this kind takes up a lot of land.

The use of the land is carefully planned in most tribal societies in Africa. It is usually the job of the village chief to allocate land to each family or clan for clearing and use. Disputes are settled by a village meeting. The land is cleared by the men by burning, and the crops are planted and tended by the women. The crops vary according to the climate and the tradition of the area. Yams, cassava, maize, sorghum, millet, wheat, cotton and various kinds of vegetables are widely grown.

This kind of farming has been practised for thousands of years, and has sustained the human population until recently. However, subsistence farming yields only a tiny surplus each year to sell or exchange, leaving little protection against famine if the harvest is bad.

Domesticated and wild animals

The other main type of farming practised in the savannas is the raising of livestock, especially cattle. Many small farmers in Africa keep cattle as a sign of wealth, as well as for food. Cattle are also important in South America and Australia, where they are kept on ranches for large-scale meat production. In Africa, too, there are some places where cattle are raised on ranches, for example in Zimbabwe, Botswana, South Africa and Tanzania, but the ranchers encounter many difficulties. One of the most important is disease.

The wild animals of Africa are immune to many diseases that domesticated cattle can catch. As the wild animals evolved, they built up a natural resistance to many of the

△ The Masai people, who live mostly in Kenya and Tanzania, rear cattle on the grasslands.

tropical diseases. However, cattle came originally from the Middle East and Europe, so they are not naturally adapted to a tropical environment. They are susceptible to foot and mouth disease, sleeping sickness and many parasites. It has been suggested by ecologists that it would be better if the people of the savanna lands herded the naturally healthy populations of wild animals and domesticated them, instead of trying to rear expensive cattle. Perhaps this will happen as people begin to realise how valuable the wild animals can be as food, as

a source of produce to sell, as an attraction for tourists, and as a way of conserving the grasslands.

More people, more risk

In some parts of Africa and South America the population is growing very quickly. The number of people in the African countries of Kenya and Zimbabwe increases by over four per cent a year compared to only 0.5 per cent in western Europe and the USA. This means that more food must be produced, and in some areas of subsistence farming the land has to be re-used before the natural vegetation can put back the plant food. If the people cannot afford fertilisers to feed the soil, the crop yields begin to fall, increasing the risk of famine. As the land becomes over-cropped, or over-grazed by cattle, the soil begins to disintegrate. The soil is either washed away by heavy rain or blown away by the wind. These risks are highest in areas of low and unreliable rainfall, because the rain in these areas usually comes in torrential downpours, often in thunderstorms.

For the last two decades the rains have been unreliable in the Sahel region. The shrinking rainfall has meant that many areas bordering the Sahara have been abandoned altogether as the desert has advanced. Some scientists think that the desert claims another nine kilometres of land every year. Once-prosperous villages have been overwhelmed by shifting sand, or have been reduced to mounds of clay as the mud-brick houses have fallen apart. Many scientists are now trying to find out the reasons for the failure of the rains.

In the 1970s and 80s terrible famines occurred in a particular stretch of the savannas in Africa known as the Sahel zone (see map on page 4). The Sahel lies between the arid lands of the Sahara, and the savannas with higher rainfall to the south.

▽ Drought has led to soil erosion in Burkina Faso.

A change in climate

About 100 years ago some scientists suggested that burning coal, oil and gas for fuel would eventually affect the climate of the world. Many scientists now think that this prediction is true. When fossil fuels are burned they produce gases, especially carbon dioxide, which trap the heat radiated from the Earth. As more heat is retained the air gradually heats up and climates across the world become warmer. This is called the 'greenhouse effect'.

Most of the warming is expected to happen in the middle and high latitudes. Tropical lands will become only slightly hotter. However, even the smallest rise of average temperatures has a noticeable effect on the wind systems of the world. Rain-bearing winds are less likely to reach the drier parts of the savannas.

The changes in climate will produce changes in vegetation and conditions for people and animals. We need to be able to measure these changes in order to plan ahead. The most advanced measuring is being done by scientists in the United States, where they have devised an ingenious way to look at the Earth.

Every colour tells a story

All objects give off energy in the form of waves. Scientists can analyse the wavelengths of different types of energy by using an instrument called a spectroscope. The American scientists have mounted a spectroscopic camera on a U2 spyplane. The U2 flies over the savannas and photographs their vegetation at different wavelengths. From the colour of the pictures, the scientists can tell what is happening to the vegetation, even down to the health of an individual tree. A tree which is suffering because of lack of water gives different wavelengths from those given off by a healthy tree.

The pictures taken by the spectroscopic camera are so accurate that it is possible to predict whether an individual tree will die in the next five years. This kind of information will help scientists to predict the regions where people are likely to be affected by famine.

Animals of the savannas

The primary consumers

In an environment where plants and animals live together, ecologists call all the animals that eat the plants 'primary consumers'. It does not matter whether they are birds, mammals or insects, if they eat green plants they are primary consumers. In turn, animals that feed off the plant-eaters are 'secondary consumers'. The savannas provide huge quantities of food for both groups. However, the energy contained in the plants cannot pass from plant to animal, and from animal to animal, unchanged.

Animals use up energy as they graze for their food, chew it and digest it. In fact, they use so much energy doing these things that only about 10 per cent of the energy contained in the plants eaten by the animals is actually used for their growth. In the same way, when a meat-eater such as a cheetah or an eagle chases its prey, it needs a lot of energy to catch it. Once again, only about 10 per cent of the energy contained in the food is actually used for growth. Therefore, the number of animals – primary or secondary consumers – that can survive is always limited by this 10 per cent rule. In most **ecosystems** there are usually at least 10 times more primary than secondary consumers.

This rule applies to all environments – except human ones. We have overcome it by farming the land, breeding new crops, using fertilisers, watering the land by irrigation, and eliminating pests and weeds. All these agricultural methods create an artificial ecosystem in which the energy available to humans from plants is much greater than it would be in a natural ecosystem.

Insects and birds

The larger animals are important primary consumers of the grass in the savannas. However, they are not necessarily the main primary consumers. Even the largest herds of grazing animals cannot keep pace with the appetites of some of the major insect and bird groups. A single locust swarm can contain over 1,000 million insects. A swarm like this can eat over 3,000 tonnes of green plants a day. The more common leaf-feeding insects, such as leaf cutter ants, are much less destructive. Their numbers are usually in balance with the amount of food available.

Almost as destructive as locusts are some of the bird species. In Africa one species of the weaverbird gathers in the dry season in flocks of several millions. These migrate from place to place consuming huge amounts of seeds, including seeds sown for crops by the farmers. They also nest in colonies of millions of pairs in the wet season. Less destructive seed-eaters include doves, bustards, larks and pipits. Other birds have become adapted to a life on the ground, and survive by excellent camouflage and by being able to run quite fast. They include the guineafowl, bustard, rhea, emu,

▷ When locusts (main picture) swarm in their millions (inset) they can strip the land bare.
▽ Leafcutter ants

△ An ostrich male with two females

▽ Golden-backed weaver

and the largest living bird, the ostrich.

In addition to all the local species, the savannas of the Americas and Africa are used by many winter migrants fleeing the cold of Canada and the United States, Europe and northern Asia. For example, the grasslands of Africa provide a temporary home for swallows, wheatears, kestrels, black kites, spoonbills, cranes, owls and many others.

The underground feeders

As well as the leaves, stalks and seeds above ground, another important source of food for the primary consumers is the root growth of the grasses, below ground. A huge number of insects, earthworms, bacteria and fungi feed on live and dead root material (humus). There are also larger animals that plunder this underground food store. In Africa and South America these are the rodents, such as the vizcacha and the desert rat. The rabbit was introduced by the Europeans into Australia and South America, but there are native 'rabbits' (actually members of the

△ The jack rabbit, really a hare, feeds on grass leaves and roots.

hare family) in both the African and American savannas.

Studies have shown how important litter-feeders are for the plants of the savannas. In one study in Nigeria the underground-feeding termites ate 60 per cent of the wood litter, 60 per cent of the grass litter and three per cent of the leaf litter of a dry savanna region. In a wetter area, earthworms consumed about the same percentages of the non-woody litter. In fact, many ecologists think that all these feeders are more important plant consumers than the larger animals. Even the animals in big grazing herds may eat only one tenth of all the food available.

The delicate balance

The ecology of the plants and animals of the savanna is very complex. In fact, the balance of nature in these lands is one of the most delicate of all the world's environments. It is only recently that scientists have begun to study it in detail. One of the most important things they have learned is that when people and their farming systems move into the savanna in large numbers the balance can be very easily damaged. There are also many dangers to human life if the ecological rules of the savanna are broken.

People are now very poor primary consumers of the savannas, even though it is where our ancestors evolved and flourished.

ecosystem – a group of plants and animals that share the same environment.

The cool grasslands

Prairies, steppes and pampas

Most of the regions that used to be covered by the cool grasslands are now under cultivation. Only the drier edges of these lands still retain grass-covered areas similar to the original grasslands. These areas are found in the western United States and Canada, central Asia, parts of Australia, and southern Argentina – but even here the original animals have largely disappeared. Nevertheless, it is still important to understand the original ecology as far as we can, because the soils of the cool grasslands have not changed. They are some of the best croplands in the world. Terrible mistakes have been made in the past with these soils because people did not understand their ecology. They had no idea what would happen to them if they were ploughed, or grazed too hard.

North America and Asia

The grasses that dominate the cool grasslands have deep roots and can resist drought. They are mostly different from the grasses of the hot grasslands and grow mixed with many other herbaceous (non-woody) **annuals, perennials** and bulb plants, as well as low woody shrubs. Where rainfall is abundant, there are tall grass formations, around one or two metres high.

▽ Prairie grasslands are preserved in the Yellowstone National Park, USA.

△ The people of Kazakhstan, who live on the steppe grasslands of Asia, migrate to where rain produces good grazing for their animals.

Where there is less rainfall, the grass is shorter. In very dry areas, the grass is only a few centimetres high – for example, buffalo grass and grama in North America. Under these three main grass formations lie three different soil types.

The climates of the grasslands are very varied. In North America, grasslands originally stretched unbroken from Alberta in Canada almost to the Gulf of Mexico in Texas. This huge area includes many different climates. There are intensely cold winters in the north, and hot, thundery summers with mild winters in the far south. Yet the same species are found across the whole region. How the same species can grow in such widely differing climates was always a great puzzle, until modern research uncovered the answer.

Grass races

Although the grasses may all belong to the same species, they have different races. Just as people belong to different races with different **genes**, so there are races in most other kinds of living things. In the grasslands, the genes that allow species to survive cold will dominate in the regions with a cold climate. Those genes that give species a strong resistance to heat and drought will dominate in the areas with a hot climate.

For a time, as the ice age came to an end 12,000 to 10,000 years ago, grasslands became more widespread than before in both North America and Asia. In North America there were grasslands reaching almost as far as the Atlantic coast and the Great Lakes. The edge of this 'prairie peninsula' retreated as the forest advanced. By 2,000 years ago it was practically the same as the Europeans found it, when they explored the interior of the continent 1,500 years later.

South America, Africa and Australia

The cool grasslands of the southern continents have many features which make

them different from the northern grasslands. The grassy plains of Argentina and Uruguay, known as pampas, were originally dominated by only one major grass type, the tall feather grasses. Hardly any of this kind of landscape is left now because the original grasses have been replaced by grasses grown for grazing. In South Africa, the **veld** joins up with the hot savannas, as do the cooler and hotter grasslands of Australia. Many of the grass species, as well as the wild animals, are common to both hot and cool areas in these continents.

Predators and prey in the prairies and steppes

The number of different animal species in the cool grasslands of North America is not large. There are only 20 species of animal larger than a dog, compared to over 80 in the

◁ Pampas (inset) is now only found at the drier edges of the cool grasslands in South America (top: Chile). It has disappeared from the hot grasslands (bottom: Brazil).
▽ Prairie dogs live in huge colonies.

African savannas. Many of the animal types of North America, such as mastodons and camels, became extinct at the end of the last ice age. Nevertheless, before the European settlement of North America, the actual number of animals was huge. Estimates suggest that over 50 million buffalo roamed across the prairies in their long migrations from north to south. There were also millions of deer, pronghorn 'antelope', ground-living birds like the prairie chicken and grouse, and smaller mammals such as the jackrabbit and the prairie dog (also called marmot).

Feeding on the grazing animals were the carnivores such as owls, eagles and hawks. But the main predator was the grey wolf. Before it was exterminated in many parts of North America and Asia, this animal was the most widespread mammal in the world, apart from humans. In Asia its main prey on the grasslands was the saiga antelope and the wild horse. In the 1980s, some ecologists suggested that the grey wolf should be re-introduced into some of the unfarmed western grasslands of the United States. It would save a lot of money by hunting animals which are, at the moment, shot in order to keep their numbers under control. The suggestion was met with horror by the local people!

Unlike the savannas, where most grazers prefer one sort of food to another, the animals of the steppes and prairies fed on whatever was available. Fortunately, the hot winds of summer turned the grass into natural hay, providing food throughout the year. The eating habits of the huge herds, helped by fire, kept down tree growth. Occasionally, a tree would survive on the flat lands but most were confined to the rivers or damper hollows.

Soils

Most of the soils beneath the prairies are deep and very dry. The long roots of the grasses extend down over a metre but near the surface the roots are densely twined together. Mixed in with them are tough lower leaves, and the two together form a thick matting or 'sod'. This is almost impossible for water to penetrate. Water which does enter, for example from melting snow, is held as if in a sponge. Some runs down the numerous earthworm burrows, but much of the movement of water in summer is upwards from below as the sun causes underground water to evaporate.

The root matting not only prevents water from entering the soil, but also slows down the penetration of air. The roots, and the numerous earthworms and insects that eat the dead grass litter, generate a lot of carbon dioxide in the soil. The litter-eaters are so numerous that they reduce the dead plant remains to minerals very efficiently. Among the minerals they release from the dead plants is one called calcium. This reacts with the carbon dioxide to make lime (calcium carbonate). The lime collects in old earthworm burrows, or forms into nodules turning the soil a black, or dark brown colour. The Russian name for these black soils is *chernozem*. Scientists use this name worldwide for the darkest prairie soil.

Grain on the grasslands

The European settlers quickly found that the soils of the cool grassland areas were ideal for grass crops such as wheat and maize. The natural grasslands could also feed large herds of cattle and sheep. In the 19th and 20th centuries, in the United States, Canada,

Fires help to release plant food which is contained in the old dead grass, and which helps plant growth when the spring rains come.

Most of the hoofed animals can escape from grassland fires quite easily, and many of the others are unhurt underground.

Indian summer

Just as in the savannas, frequent fires in the cool grasslands help to prevent the growth of woody plants. Many of the fires are natural, but in Asia and North America some areas were once burned regularly to encourage the growth of new grass. In North America this was a deliberate policy of the plains Indians, who depended for their food, shelter and clothing on buffalo meat and hides. The autumn pall of smoke with a hazy sunlight filtering through became known as an 'Indian summer' to the European settlers.

△ American farmers were forced to abandon their land when drought hit the prairies in the 1930s.

Argentina, Uruguay and Australia, the land was settled first by ranchers and later by farmers. The soils of the grasslands began to yield huge amounts of grain, beef, hides and wool which were exported to feed the growing cities of the industrial areas. At first, the best-watered lands with the richest soils were settled. But as more people arrived, the farmers began to cultivate the drier parts of the grasslands. It was then that the dangers of cultivation were revealed.

'Dust bowls'

The first catastrophe was in the United States. In the 1930s, drought in the drier prairies of the western Great Plains (see map page 4) caused the crops to fail. The bare soil which had been ploughed up began to blow away because the matting cover was no longer there to protect it from the wind. Enormous dust storms completely swept the soil from large areas, and many people were made homeless. Some areas became arid 'dust bowls'. In other areas with more rain, the prairie soils began to wash away because farmers had spent little money on fertilisers to replace the natural plant food from the grassland soil. Deep gulleys appeared and whole slopes began to wash into the rivers.

In an attempt to save the soils and the farms, the American government passed strict laws to change the farming methods. It also set up a soil conservation service to devise new farming methods which would suit the prairie soils. By the 1950s, over three quarters of all farmland in the country was covered by federal conservation laws. These steps saved some of the world's richest farming land. At the heart of this soil conservation was the understanding of their ecology. For the first time ever, the world could see that conservation of a natural resource like soil was both possible and necessary.

The same problems of soil erosion were experienced in Australia in the 1940s, and in the USSR in the 1960s. In both countries dust bowls appeared as the soil was eroded by wind and rain. The USSR began ploughing up ancient grassland in central Asia in the late 1950s. Within 10 years much of the topsoil had gone. To make matters worse, the dust blew westwards on to the steppes in southern Russia, killing the crops there as well. Exactly the same mistakes were made here as had been made in the USA. In 1990 the Australian government announced that it would be spending 570 million dollars to combat soil erosion. These countries, with some of the best soils in the world, are still learning the lessons of the experience of the American farmers: good farming means good ecology.

Conservation tactics

Soil conservation is only one aspect of the conservation effort in the United States and Canada. Local communities that together own over a million hectares of forest, grassland, desert, lakes, saltmarshes and rivers are helping to protect these environments. There are also many societies concerned with conservation. The Audubon Society in the United States, for example, helped the buffalo to survive. The remnants of the once-great herds, only a few hundred animals, were rounded up and moved to an area of grassland in Colorado, where they were protected and managed. The herd now numbers several thousand. A similar project was undertaken in Canada.

Protecting animals is easier than protecting vegetation. Saving grassland in populated areas is probably the most difficult of all conservation work. One example is the long grass prairie which was the first to be settled and farmed. One type of long grass prairie, dominated by the big blue stem grass, originally covered about 100,000 square kilometres in the state of Illinois alone. A survey in the 1980s showed only 10 square kilometres left in the state. Ecologists and local people began to hunt for the many species that lived among the grasses.

They found that the plants had survived in some places such as old pioneer cemeteries, often not mown for years, and railway track sides. They began to collect the seeds by hand and send them to the University of Illinois. Altogether about 300 kilograms were sent. The University looked for a site big enough to recreate the big blue stem prairie. For this they needed thousands of hectares. They found 2,753 hectares where nobody would want to live – or even be allowed to live – on top of the University's underground atom research laboratory.

The greenhouse threat

We have already seen the threat from the greenhouse effect to the savannas (see page 21). The same threat of increasing drought exists in the cool grasslands. In the 1980s, droughts in the American prairie lands reduced many farmers to poverty. The worst affected lands managed to survive by tapping underground water to irrigate the land by spraying. However, as the rainfall decreases the ground water is beginning to run out. In several states in the mid-west region there are large areas dependent on only one main ground source, called the Ogallala Aquifer. Many farms have been abandoned and much of the land has returned to short, buffalo grass prairie. It has even been suggested that it would be better to pay off the farmers and bring back the buffalo. These could be reared on ranches and the meat exported at a cheap price. The hides would also be valuable as fine leather. In Texas, farming deer has proved very successful, so why not buffalo?

Scientists cannot say for certain if the droughts are a result of the greenhouse effect, or whether they will continue regularly. But if the prairies do become drier, this will be a serious threat to the food supply for the whole world. The population of the world will increase to over 7,000 from just over 5,000 million by the year 2020. Food surpluses, particularly from the American prairies, already keep much of the world from starvation in bad harvest emergencies. If production falls because of a change in climate we will need all the ecological knowledge we have learned about the cool grasslands to overcome this problem. Other countries that farm the cool grasslands, such as the USSR, will also need to make efforts to reach the same standards of farming as in the United States. It is a tragedy that some of the best soil nature has provided should be so badly used.

▷ Buffalo herds are adapted to the climate and vegetation of the cool grasslands where they live.

annuals – plants that complete their life cycle in one year.
perennials – plants that live for several years.
genes – units of heredity that determine characteristics such as eye colour.
veld – grassland in southern Africa.

People take over

In the beginning

Scientists have been convinced for over 100 years that human beings evolved from savanna grassland apes. More than one human-ape developed, but the earlier types became extinct. Evidence from fossils and body chemistry (the proteins of which we are made) seems to show the line of evolution that led to creatures like us beginning about five million years ago. Modern human beings (*Homo sapiens*) appeared about 100,000 years ago. They quickly spread to all parts of the world from their original home, probably the African savannas. About 400,000 years before this, our more ancient ancestors (*Homo erectus*) had learned the control of fire. From that time on human beings had an increasing impact on nature.

People and fire

In a narrow valley in the Guardarrama mountains of central Spain, the skeletons of many large animals, such as rhino and elephant, have been found. The evidence shows that these animals had run into a swamp which filled the valley floor, about 300,000 years ago. As the animals sank into the deep mud of the swamp they were killed by humans, and cut up for food. The people had driven the animals into the swamp by lighting fires. Firing grassland to trap animals probably expanded the total area of the world's grasslands in both hot and cool lands over thousands of years. It is now often difficult to say whether a grassland is natural

▽ Grassland on South Island, New Zealand, may have been produced by burning woodland.

△ The life style of the Tukano Indians is threatened as their land is taken over for cattle ranches.

or manmade. In New Zealand, for example, grassy areas like the Canterbury Plains on South Island existed when the Europeans first arrived. But unlike most grassland areas, there was no dry season. Most people think that these grasslands were formed as a result of the Maori people setting fire to them, and gradually killing off the trees. In fact, in all the grassland regions the presence of people and their fires is one of the most important parts of the ecology.

Not only did people affect the grasslands by setting fire to them for hunting. About 10,000 years ago, humans also learned how to cultivate some of the grasses. Wheat and barley were domesticated in the Middle East, maize in the Americas, rice in south-east Asia and millet in China. At around the same time people began to keep animals like cattle, sheep, goats, llamas and camels. Clearing the land for ploughing and grazing also increased the areas of grassland country.

Saving our heritage

People have been altering the ecology of the world's grasslands for thousands of years. The animals that share the grassland environment with us have been greatly affected by these changes. Until recently the ways of life of many human groups were in balance with the resources of their environments. They did not need extensive areas for farming, so much wild land remained untouched. They used spears, blowpipes, bows and arrows and fire to catch limited numbers of animals. On the whole, they rarely took more animals than their tribal customs dictated.

In some tribal societies, such as those of the American Indians, hunting was part of the religious and social life. In Colombia, research by scientists who study human societies has shown that tribes like the Tukano Indians have a very clear idea of the animal and plant resources of the areas in which they live. They also understand the ecology of their environment. They know how energy from the sun flows through the system from plant to animal to people, and what each species needs in order to flourish. This knowledge is the basis of their religion, and they see themselves as part of the ecological system, just like the animals they hunt and the plants they eat.

Conservation as a way of life

For the Tukano Indians, conservation is a natural part of their way of life. They know that the resources of the environment are limited. If too much is taken out of the forest and grassland, the energy of the system will decline and they will harm themselves. Sadly, they believe that this energy is now running down. In the past there were more animals, fruits and fish than now. Even though they attempt to renew the energy of their environment by ceremonies, they are aware that resources are scarcer.

Their environment is being affected by changes in the way the land is used in territory around them. Large areas of the savannas of Colombia have been turned into cattle farms, and forest has been chopped down and burned to clear land for the same

35

△ The Ngorogoro Crater in Tanzania is one of the greatest reserves of wild animals in the whole of Africa.

purpose. Hunters, and people who gather forest products, have been forced to move into a smaller area, reducing the resources for their traditional way of life. As a result, the wild animal and plant life is gradually disappearing.

The story of the Tukano Indians is similar to that of many other once-wild parts of the world. The only hope for the survival of ways of life like the Tukano's is for the people of the world to find new ways to live with the wildlife of the planet. Conservation must be as much a part of the way of life for all the world's people as it is for the Tukano.

A world conservation plan

In 1982, a National Parks world conference was held, in which most of the countries of the world took part. It was agreed that by 1992, 10 per cent of the world's wild land should be protected in reserves and parks. Unfortunately, this target will not be reached. Only about four per cent will be protected by this date. There are many reasons for this failure.

Much of the wild land is in the poorer countries of Africa, Asia and South America. These countries use all their money simply trying to feed and employ their populations and keep them healthy. Spending money on wild land and animals is not given a high priority. Even where large areas of land are designated 'nature reserves' or 'parks', these are often simply areas on a map. There are not enough resources to employ people to manage and run them properly. The local people may go on killing animals as they have always done. As the human population rises, the numbers of animals killed increases. Poachers come in and kill

△ Spotted hyena. Hyenas are one of the most efficient hunters in Africa.

high, lush and coarse. The elephant, hippo and buffalo herds move into this and feast on it. As they are heavy animals, they smash down much of the grass and trample it flat. When the water begins to dry up and the bulky food has gone, they migrate elsewhere for food. The grass then puts out new lower shoots which the smaller animals like the eland, zebra, hartebeest and topi antelope eat. Finally, as this is used up and the cool season drought begins, animals like the Thompson's gazelle, which can eat coarse dry fodder, move in. The gazelles need only a little drinking water to survive, so the lack of surface water is not a great disadvantage.

A third check which helps the balance of the ecosystem is provided by the predators that eat the grazing animals. The younger, older, or less strong males live solitary lives at the outer edges of the herd. The central mass of the herd is made up of the females, their young and the dominant male. Consequently, it is the isolated animals which tend to be killed most often by the predators. As they are not important to breeding, their loss does not affect the future of the herd, even if quite a number are killed.

Research also shows that the predators themselves have natural checks which keep their numbers in balance. Lions have been found to live in groups (prides) of up to 10 individuals, but almost never more than this. The extra male lions are forced to live out of the prides, so their chances of survival and breeding are less. In wild dog packs, the dominant female usually kills off the puppies of other females, so only one litter is allowed to survive. The fastest of the predators, the cheetah is known now to have a very poor breeding record. Barely one in twenty of its cubs reaches adulthood. All these checks ensure that the hunters are kept in balance with the hunted, and that neither group destroys the system which sustains them all.

When people interfere with the environment of the animals then these delicate balances can be easily upset. Road building, farming, grazing, land enclosure, land drainage, reservoir building, mining, hunting and poaching can all disrupt the ecology of the animals and their environment. In the Serengeti Park in northern Tanzania poaching of leopards for their skins, and cheetah cubs for smuggling to collectors, has upset the balance so that the grazing herds have increased. This is affecting the growth of the grasses, and more bushes and scrub are colonising the land.

Many scientists and game managers now feel that much more active management is needed to maintain the ecosystem. In 1990, ecologists from London Zoo who work in Africa proposed that in areas like Tanzania, Kenya, Zimbabwe and Zambia there should be a system of managed hunting. It would replace the predators, like the leopard and cheetah, which have been reduced in number. The kills would be selective, just like those of the natural predators, except they would be chosen by the game wardens and scientists. The licence to shoot the game would be expensive, and would bring in much more money than the illegal selling of skins and tusks. Hunting would also provide employment for local people as guides and camp helpers. Many of the governments are enthusiastic about the idea, but some wildlife organisations are against it. To some people killing for pleasure, and not saving animals from being hunted, seems a backward step. However, there are successful examples in other areas of the world where controlled hunting has preserved the animal life.

In North America the pronghorn 'antelope', which was once common from Mexico to Canada, was hunted down by 1910 to a few small scattered groups. Emergency protection allowed its numbers to increase once more, and it is now numerous in Wyoming and Montana especially. However, its natural predator, the grey wolf, has been eliminated. The place of the wolf has been taken by the sporting hunter under careful control of the state wildlife services, so its future is assured.

In the USSR and Mongolia the saiga antelope, like the pronghorn, was hunted almost to extinction. By 1920 only a few hundred survived of the herds of many thousands. The government protected the animals, and their numbers stayed about the same for 20 to 30 years. Then in the 1940s the animals began to spread once more. Within a decade a rough count showed that there were 700,000 antelope in Asia, and 50,000 in the European steppes. By 1960 there were around two million saiga antelope in the USSR. The rapidity of the rise was a result of the Soviet government's campaign to eliminate the wolf. Thousands of people were employed to kill wolves in the 1940s, 50s, and 60s – so the saiga increased rapidly. There were so many of them that they began to destroy the grassland vegetation, allowing wind erosion to blow the soil away. To balance their numbers the government allowed controlled hunting once more. Soviet ecologists monitor the herds of these small animals (they are under one metre high) and estimates suggest they are now around one million in number. Their hides, meat and bones can be sold.

In Africa there are a number of animal species which are facing the same threat of extinction as the pronghorn and saiga once did. In northern Angola the magnificent sable antelope is down to a population of

△ Pronghorn antelope

only a few hundred. This large animal is prized for its huge curved horns which can grow to over a metre long. In Senegal, Mali and Guinea the giant eland is under threat, not only because of its hides and good meat, but also as a result of the increasing drought in the region which has affected it badly. In both cases it has been suggested that the animals should be semi-domesticated in order to supply meat, hides and horn for consumption and trade. Experiments are also being made to domesticate various other animals of the savannas, especially in East Africa. It is hoped that one day local people may regard the savanna wild stock with as much pride as they feel for their beloved cattle.

Saving the wild horses

The most successful domestication of all the grassland animals is that of the horse. At least 5,000 years ago, the people of Central Asia tamed the ancestors of our modern horses. The animals, and the techniques of using them both in war and peace, soon spread throughout Eurasia. In the Republic of Mongolia itself horses are still herded and used in traditional ways. The people migrate with their horses in search of good fodder on the harsh steppelands. This way of life has survived because of the wealth produced by the trading of horses.

The original wild horses and asses of Asia have now almost gone. The last few of one species, the shaggy-coated Przewalski's horse, were saved by Russian and Polish naturalists in the 19th century. About 1,000 of these animals are in zoos round the world. In 1991, the London Zoo and other British zoos, together with the Mongolian government, returned some Przewalski's horses to the Altai-Gobi National Park in Mongolia. They will be kept in fenced steppeland until their numbers increase, then set loose to roam free. The Mongolian people regard this animal as a national symbol. Its return would cause great joy.

Hope for the future

It is by generating wealth for the local people that the best hope lies for saving the animals of the grasslands. The Tukano of South America use their *shaman's* wisdom to maintain the natural balance of their environment. We need the wisdom of our modern *shamans* – scientists, economists, business people and governments – to do likewise. We also need the co-operation of all the ordinary people who think that it is important for the future health of the planet that the grassland system should survive. After all, it was our original homeland.

▽ The Przewalski's horse (inset: mare and foal), once common in Mongolia (main picture) was saved from extinction in zoos in Europe. Now it is being reintroduced to the wild in Mongolia.

Animals in danger

△ An ivory worker in Hong Kong

In the last two decades, the destruction of the rich fauna of the grasslands, especially in Africa, has been well documented. Many countries and individual organisations are working hard to save what is left of the last wildernesses on Earth. One spectacular example from many will illustrate both the dangers of conservation, and what is being achieved.

The fate of the elephants

In 1981, there were 1.2 million elephants on the African continent. In 1990, their numbers had fallen to 750,000. There are a number of reasons for this dramatic fall in the elephant population. First and foremost is poaching for the ivory trade. During the 1980s the trade in ivory expanded. This expansion was to supply the ivory trinket-makers of Hong Kong who sold to the tourists, and exported their goods to Europe and Japan.

A second important reason is that the elephants are not popular animals with the farmers of Africa. One farmer in Botswana said in 1989: 'We in Katchibau love all animals. They have been with us since we were born. There are only three animals we dislike: elephants because they threaten our crops; lions because they eat our livestock; and snakes because we do not eat them.'

▽ An elephant herd in Namibia

It is certainly true that elephants are very destructive, and not only of crops. Elephants need large amounts of calcium to keep their huge bones healthy. They find this in tree bark, and kill many trees by stripping and eating their bark. In Uganda, in the Kabelega Falls National Park, an elephant herd destroyed nearly all the trees during the 1960s and 70s. What had been a dense woodland savanna was transformed into an open savanna in only 20 years because the elephant herds were protected. To many local people, the elephants are pests. By destroying the trees they reduce the supply of fuel for essential things like cooking. To take their ivory by poaching is a good way of making money, and of getting rid of them at the same time.

In 1990, the trade in ivory was banned. Huge stocks of tusks were destroyed and poaching was no longer profitable. But elephants could still be in danger. Before the ban was enforced, some African countries argued that without some trade, the farmers would have no reason to conserve the elephant herds at all. The ban might even lead to a faster fall in the elephant population as the herds were exterminated by the farmers. Thankfully, this has not happened. Now, some African countries, together with international agencies and countries like Britain and Belgium, are planning to manage the herds.

To do this means confining the animals to areas of land which can support them, so that they don't interfere with the people and their crops. The numbers of elephants will also be controlled to allow trees to establish themselves. Control means selective killing (culling) of the males, so the herds retain their vigour. From the males will come the ivory to be exported. There will also be a supply of meat, hides and bones for local people. Elephant management could produce income for the African countries, and provide attraction for the growing tourist trade. The farmers will be able to supply food for visitors, as well as finding employment in hotels and transport. This kind of management is already working very successfully in South Africa.

△ Carved tusks for sale

Farming problems

The difficulties of designing and managing reserves can be seen in one of the most important African game reserves, sited on the Okavango swamp in northern Botswana. This area is a unique inland river delta which floods in the wet season. Vast numbers of wild animals of all kinds travel long distances to feed and breed there. In the centre of the country is another reserve – an area of savanna grassland. Together the two cover over 60,000 square kilometres. This is nearly one fifth of the area of the whole of Botswana. However, the animals use the swamp area only in the summer, when food is abundant in the wet season. In the dry season they migrate long distances to better feeding grounds. It is on these migrations that the elephants, for example, do most damage.

The main farming in Botswana is cattle raising. As the wild animals migrate they carry diseases like foot and mouth, rinderpest, ticks and worms on to land reserved for the cattle. They also break down fences built to protect and control the cattle. All this costs the farmers money. Their support for the conservation of the wild animals used to be strong, but is now becoming less enthusiastic. In Botswana, despite the reserves, the numbers of wild animals are still falling, as many are killed by the farmers, or kept from good feeding grounds. In an opinion poll taken in the country in 1989, two thirds of the people agreed with the statement 'Cattle are more important than wildlife'.

△ A Masai boy tends a herd of cattle on grassland in Kenya.

In future, reserves must be planned to fit the ecology of both animals and people. One proposal is to make corridor areas linking the reserves so that animals can move around without interfering with the farmers. Another plan is to plant many more trees to increase the variety of places to live for animals, and to help conserve water. The most ambitious scheme of this kind is to grow green belts of trees around the Sahara and Kalahari deserts in the drier savannas.

Around the world there are over 400 million hectares of protected natural lands. Many of these parks and reserves include people as well. The parks and reserves will only work if people are part of the plans. To achieve this balance is the aim of the World Biodiversity Project, set up in 1989. This project will assemble masses of information, and produce plans for most of the world's wilderness landscapes. It is a huge task. In 1990, the Sierra Club of the United States analysed maps made from space by the American military. They estimated about one third of the Earth's land is still wilderness. Of this huge area only about one fifth has some kind of protection.

To extend our protection to nature, and manage the Earth so that it sustains itself, its animals and its plants, will be one of the major tasks of the 21st century, requiring more and more accurate knowledge. Ecologists in the United States have agreed to set up long-term research projects. These are designed to monitor what is happening to the world's ecosystems over 100 years. Each major ecosystem, like the savannas and the prairies, will be monitored both on the ground and from space. The information will be analysed by special computer programmes. This is 'ecowatching' on a grand scale, but it is only the beginning.

It is estimated that, at present, one quarter of all the world's plants and animals are in danger of extinction. If this tragedy is to be avoided, it requires everyone – not just scientists – to be involved in saving the Earth's living resources. Human beings evolved and survived on the savannas because of their superior brain power. It is up to all of us to show that our superior brains are capable of taking the Earth's living resources with us into the future. We are all 'ecowatchers' now.